The Man Who Missed Christmas
by J. Edgar Parks.
Reprinted with permission from Guideposts Magazine.
Copyright 1955 by Guideposts, Carmel, NY.
Francie Nolan's Christmas Tree, from A Tree Grows in Brooklyn by Betty Smith.
Copyright 1943, 1947 by Betty Smith. Copyright renewed 1971 by Betty Smith (Finch).
Reprinted by permission of HarperCollins Publishers, Inc.
A Faraway Christmas excerpt from *My Christmas Treasury* by Norman Vincent Peale.
Copyright 1991 Ruth S. Peale Marital Trust.
Reprinted by permission of HarperCollins Publishers, Inc.
A Santa's Suit Does Not a Santa Make, from Seven Stories of Christmas Love
by Leo Buscaglia. Reprinted by permission.
Christmas Day in the Morning by Pearl S. Buck.
Copyright 1955 by Pearl S. Buck. Copyright renewed 1983.
Reprinted by permission of Harold Ober Associates.
The Christmas Pageant from *It Was On Fire When I Lay Down On It*
by Robert Fulghum. Copyright © 1988, 1989 By Robert L. Fulghum.
Reprinted by permission of Villard Books, a division of Random House, Inc.

The editor and publisher have made every effort to trace the ownership of all
copyrighted material and to secure permission from copyright holders of such material.
In the event of any question arising as to the use of any material, the publisher
and editor, while expressing regret for inadvertent error, will be pleased
to make the necessary correction in future printings.

C.R. Gibson® is a registered trademark of Thomas Nelson, Inc.

Book Design: Aurora Campanella

Printed in the U.S.A.
GB950
ISBN 0-8378-7162-X

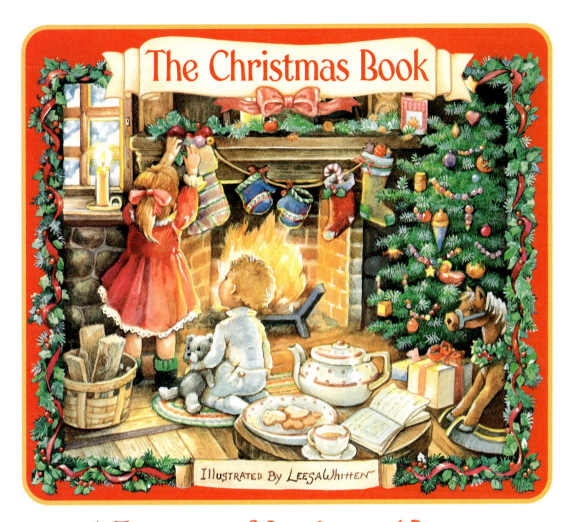

A Treasury of Stories and Poems

Compiled by Eileen Mulkerin D'Andrea
Illustrated by Leesa Whitten

The C.R. Gibson Company, Norwalk, Connecticut 06856

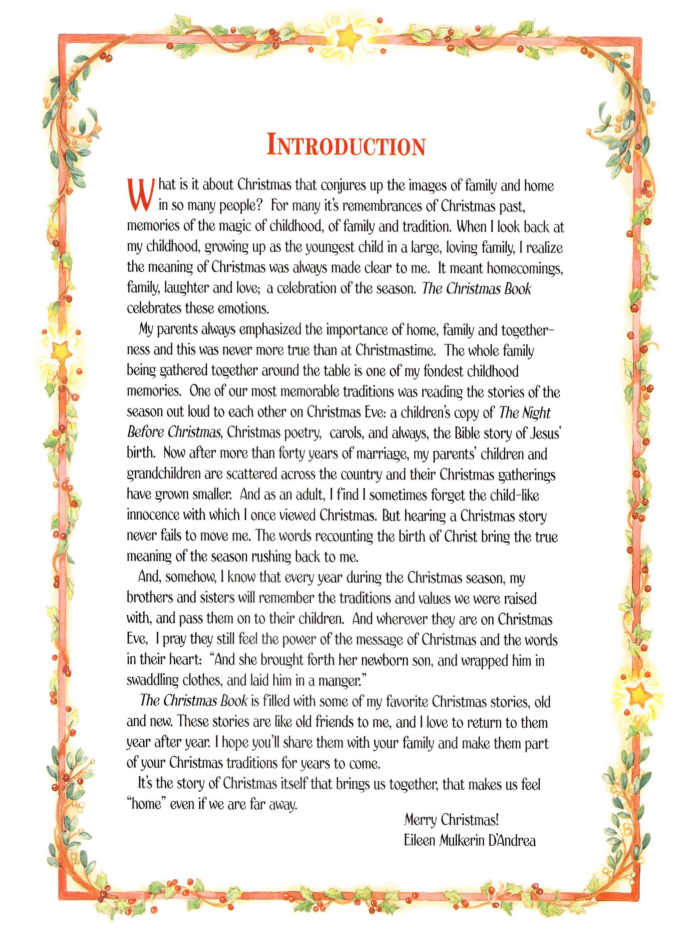

INTRODUCTION

What is it about Christmas that conjures up the images of family and home in so many people? For many it's remembrances of Christmas past, memories of the magic of childhood, of family and tradition. When I look back at my childhood, growing up as the youngest child in a large, loving family, I realize the meaning of Christmas was always made clear to me. It meant homecomings, family, laughter and love; a celebration of the season. *The Christmas Book* celebrates these emotions.

My parents always emphasized the importance of home, family and togetherness and this was never more true than at Christmastime. The whole family being gathered together around the table is one of my fondest childhood memories. One of our most memorable traditions was reading the stories of the season out loud to each other on Christmas Eve: a children's copy of *The Night Before Christmas*, Christmas poetry, carols, and always, the Bible story of Jesus' birth. Now after more than forty years of marriage, my parents' children and grandchildren are scattered across the country and their Christmas gatherings have grown smaller. And as an adult, I find I sometimes forget the child-like innocence with which I once viewed Christmas. But hearing a Christmas story never fails to move me. The words recounting the birth of Christ bring the true meaning of the season rushing back to me.

And, somehow, I know that every year during the Christmas season, my brothers and sisters will remember the traditions and values we were raised with, and pass them on to their children. And wherever they are on Christmas Eve, I pray they still feel the power of the message of Christmas and the words in their heart: "And she brought forth her newborn son, and wrapped him in swaddling clothes, and laid him in a manger."

The Christmas Book is filled with some of my favorite Christmas stories, old and new. These stories are like old friends to me, and I love to return to them year after year. I hope you'll share them with your family and make them part of your Christmas traditions for years to come.

It's the story of Christmas itself that brings us together, that makes us feel "home" even if we are far away.

Merry Christmas!
Eileen Mulkerin D'Andrea

TABLE OF CONTENTS

The Christmas Story

And it came to pass in those days, that there went out a decree from Caesar Augustus, that all the world should be taxed. (And this taxing was first made when Cyrenius was governor of Syria.) And all went to be taxed, every one into his own city. And Joseph also went up from Galilee, out of the city of Nazareth, into Judaea, unto the city of David, which is called Bethlehem; (because he was of the house and lineage of David:), to be taxed with Mary his espoused wife, being great with child.

And so it was, that, while they were there, the days were accomplished that she should be delivered. And she brought forth her firstborn son, and wrapped him in swaddling clothes, and laid him in a manger; because there was no room for them in the inn.

And there were in the same country shepherds abiding in the field, keeping watch over their flock by night. And, lo, the angel of the Lord came upon them, and the glory of the Lord shone round about them; and they were sore afraid. And the angel said unto them, Fear not: for, behold, I bring you good tidings of great joy, which shall be to all people. For unto you is born this day in the city of David a Saviour, which is Christ the Lord. And this shall be a sign unto you; Ye shall find the babe wrapped in swaddling clothes, lying in a manger.

And suddenly there was with the angel a multitude of the heavenly host praising God, and saying, Glory to God in the highest, and on earth peace, good will toward men.

And it came to pass, as the angels were gone away from them into heaven, the shepherds said one to another, Let us now go even unto Bethlehem, and see this thing which is come to pass, which the Lord hath made known unto us. And they came with haste, and found Mary, and Joseph, and the babe lying in a manger.

And when they had seen it, they made known abroad the saying which was told them concerning this child. And all they that heard it wondered at those things which were told them by the shepherds.

But Mary kept all these things, and pondered them in her heart.

And the shepherds returned, glorifying and praising God for all the things there they had heard and seen, as it was told unto them.

—Luke 2:1-20, KJV

After Jesus was born in Bethlehem, in Judea, during the time of King Herod, Magi from the east came to Jerusalem and asked, "Where is the one who has been born King of the Jews? We saw his star in the east and have come to worship him."

When King Herod heard this he was disturbed, and all Jerusalem with him. When he had called together all the people's chief priests and teachers of law, he asked them where the Christ was to be born. "In Bethlehem in Judea," they replied, "for this is what the prophet has written:

'But you, Bethlehem, in the land of Judah, are by no means least among the rulers of Judah; for out of you will come a ruler who will be the shepherd of my people Israel.'

Then Herod called the Magi secretly and found out from them the exact time the star had appeared. He sent them to Bethlehem and said, "Go and make a careful search for the child. As soon as you find him, report to me, so that I too may go and worship him."

After they had heard the king, they went on their way, and the star they had seen in the east went ahead of them until it stopped over the place where the child was. When they saw the star they were overjoyed. On coming to the house, they saw the child with his mother Mary, and they bowed down and worshiped him. Then they opened their treasures and presented him with gifts of gold and of incense and of myrrh. And having been warned in a dream not to go back to Herod, they returned to their country by another route.

—Matthew 2:1-2, NIV

Christmas Daybreak

Before the paling of the stars,
Before the winter morn,
Before the earliest cockcrow,
Jesus Christ was born:
Born in a stable,
Cradled in a manger,
In the world His hands had made,
Born a stranger.

Priest and kind lay fast asleep
In Jerusalem,
Young and old lay fast asleep
In crowded Bethlehem:
Saint and angel, ox and ass,
Kept watch together,
Before the Christmas daybreak
In the winter weather.

Jesus on His Mother's breast
In the stable cold,
Spotless Lamb of God was He,
Shepherd of the fold.
Let us kneel with Mary Maid,
With Joseph bent and hoary,
With saint and angel, ox and ass,
To hail the King of Glory.

—Christina Georgina Rossetti—

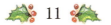

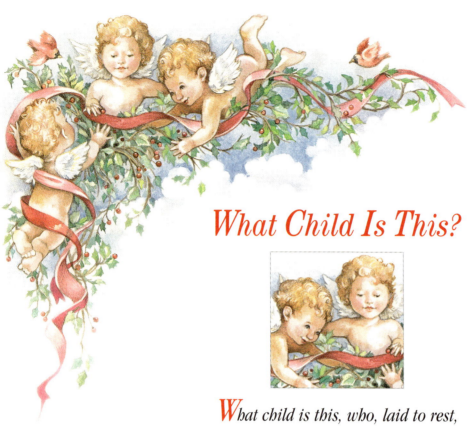

What Child Is This?

What child is this, who, laid to rest,
On Mary's lap is sleeping?
Whom angels greet with anthems sweet,
While shepherds watch are keeping?

This, this is Christ the King
Whom shepherds guard and angels sing:
Haste, haste to bring him laud,
the babe the Son of Mary.

So bring him incense, gold and myrrh,
Come, peasant, king, to own him,
The King of Kings salvation brings,
Let loving hearts enthrone him.

—W.C. Dix, c.1865—

 12

Hark! The Herald Angels Sing

Hark! the herald angels sing
Glory to the newborn King!

Peace on earth and mercy mild,
God and sinners reconciled!

Joyful, all ye nations, rise,
Join the triumph of the skies;
With angelic host proclaim
Christ is born in Bethlehem!

Hark the herald angels sing
Glory to the newborn king!

—Charles Wesley, 1739—

HOME FOR CHRISTMAS

This is meeting time again. Home is the magnet. The winter land roars and hums with the eager speed of return journeys. The dark is noisy and bright with late-night arrivals—doors thrown open, running shadows on snow, open arms, kisses, voices and laughter, laughter at everything and nothing. Inarticulate, giddying and confused are those original minutes of being back again. The very familiarity of everything acts like shock. Contentment has to be drawn in slowly, steadily, in deep breaths—there is so much of it. We rely on home not to change, and it does not, wherefore we give thanks. Again Christmas: abiding point of return. Set apart by its mystery, mood and magic, the season seems in a way to stand outside time. "All that is dear, that is lasting, renews its hold on us; we are home again…"

This glow of Christmas, has it not in it also the gold of a harvest?

"They shall return with joy, bringing their sheaves with them."

To the festival, to each other, we bring in wealth. More to tell, more to understand, more to share. Each we have garnered in yet another year; to be glad; to celebrate to the full, we are come together. How akin we are to each other, how speechlessly dear and one in the fundamentals of being, Christmas shows us. No other time grants us, quite, this vision—round the tree or gathered before the fire we perceive anew, with joy, one another's faces. And each time faces come to mean more.

Is it not one of the mysteries of life that life should, after all be so simple? Yes, as simple as Christmas, simple as this. Journeys through the dark to a lighted door, arms open. Laughter-smothered kisses, kiss-smothered laughter. And blessedness in the heart of it all. Here are the verities, all made gay with tinsel! Dear, silly Christmas-card saying and cracker mottoes—let them speak! Or, since still we cannot speak, let us sing! Dearer than memory, brighter than expectation is the ever returning now of Christmas. Why else, each time we greet its return, should happiness ring out in us like a peal of bells?

—Elizabeth Bowen

Voices in the Mist

The time draws near the birth of Christ:
The moon is high; the night is still;
The Christmas bells from hill to hill
Answer each other in the mist.

Four voices of four hamlets round,
From far and near, on mead and moor,
Swell out and fail, as if a door
Were shut between me and the sound:

Each voice four changes on the wind,
That now dilate, and now decrease,
Peace and goodwill, goodwill and peace
Peace and goodwill, to all mankind.

—Alfred, Lord Tennyson—

FARAWAY AT CHRISTMAS

Golden stars and angels. Festive lights and carols. Shoppers with gaily wrapped packages. Windows glowing with Yuletide pageantry. "Oh," a friend said to me, "aren't they wonderful, all these warm, familiar symbols? Christmas wouldn't be Christmas without them!"

I had to smile a little. Let me tell you why.

Not too long ago, my wife Ruth and the other members of our family—our three children and their spouses and assorted grandchildren—persuaded me that it would be a great adventure to spend Christmas in a completely different setting, one with a totally new atmosphere. "What if we went to Africa," they said with great excitement, "and lived in tents in one of those game parks surrounded by all those wonderful animals? Wouldn't a faraway Christmas be exciting? Wouldn't it be terrific? Wouldn't family ties be strengthened by such a unique experience?"

I protested feebly, that perhaps someone who had passed his eighty-seventh birthday, as I had, might find living in a tent surrounded by wild animals a bit strenuous. But no one seemed to be listening. "You'll love every minute of it," Ruth assured me. And so, on this high note of excitement and enthusiasm, we made our preparations to go to East Africa.

The Samburu Game Park was indeed far away. And indeed it was different. Ruth and I shared a tent pitched near a fast-flowing brown river. In tents on either side were our children and grandchildren. There was heat and dust and burning sun. At night the forest resounded with barks, screeches, splashes, and once, just behind our tents, a grunting sound that they told me the next day had probably been made by a leopard.

So I did not sleep very well, but these unfamiliar things were not what troubled me. What troubled me was that nothing seemed like Christmas. I tried to shrug off the feeling, but it persisted, a kind of emptiness, a sadness, almost, a small voice that whispered, "Christmas means coming home, doesn't it? Why have all of you chosen to turn your backs on home like this?"

I did my best to conceal such thoughts from the others, but I couldn't conceal them from myself. And they kept coming back, often at unexpected moments.

On the afternoon of Christmas Eve, for example, we had come back from a splendid day of viewing the animals. We had seen a beautiful herd of zebras, seventy-six elephants, a cheetah chasing an impala, and a nursing lioness, all magnificent in their natural surroundings. Then it was time for a shower before dinner, which was a bit of an adventure, too. The camp helpers heated water, put it in a bucket, then hoisted the bucket to the top of a pole behind the tent. From there the water ran down a pipe into the rear of the tent where, standing on slats, the bather could soap and rinse himself, after a fashion.

I was drying myself off when suddenly—I don't know what triggered it—I found myself remembering long-ago Christmases spent in Cincinnati during my impressionable boyhood years. The city was full of people of German descent, and the Germans are very sentimental about Christmas. I found myself recalling Fountain Square as it looked on Christmas Eve; I thought it the biggest, brightest, most beautiful place I had ever seen, The Christmas tree was enormous, and the streets were alive with carols, many sung in German: "*Stille Naacht*" and "*O Tannenbaum*." I could see myself walking with my father, my small hand in his big one, the snow crunching under our feet. Up on East Liberty Street, where we lived, my mother always had a tree with real candles on it. The smell of those tallow candles mingled with the scent of fir, an aroma unlike any other. Now, standing in our little tent with the vastness of Africa all around me, I remembered that wonderful smell and I missed it terribly.

We had been told there would be a special dinner for us that evening. Even this did not cheer me; I thought it might be an artificial occasion with everyone trying too hard to be merry. When I came out near dinnertime, I saw that, in the eating tent, a straggly brown bush had been set up, decorated with small colored lights and some tinsel and red ribbon. I thought of the great tree in Fountain Square and the even greater one in Rockefeller Center in New York City and the magnificent one on the great lawn of the White House in Washington.

We were called to the edge of the river, where chairs had been set up for all of us so that we could see, on the other side, two herders guarding their cattle, their spear tips gleaming like points of light in the gathering dusk. And at the peaceful, almost timeless sight, I felt something stir within me, for I knew that these herders and their charges had not

changed in thousands of years. They belonged to their landscape just as the shepherds on the hills outside Bethlehem belonged to theirs. And, at that moment, one of the grandchildren began to sing, hesitantly, tentatively, *"O Little Town of Bethlehem."* Gradually others joined in with *"Hark the Herald Angels Sing"* and then *"Joy to the World."* Soon we were all singing and, as we sang, everything seemed to change; the sense of strangeness was gone. I looked around the group—our children, their children, singing songs, sharing feelings that in a very real way went back almost 2,000 years to that simple manger in a simple town, with the herders standing by in a parched and primitive land.

Then someone began to read the immortal story from Luke: "And there were in the same country shepherds abiding in the field, keeping watch over their flock by night..." As the story went on, I thought, how wonderful and simple that only God could have thought of it.

I found myself remembering a radio talk given many years ago by Sam Shoemaker, a much-loved pastor and a good friend of mine. In it, Sam was speculating on what God the Father might have said to Jesus His Son on the night before Jesus left Him to go down to earth. He imagined Father and Son conversing much as a human boy and his father might do before the son leaves home to go out into the world. Only Sam, with his great simplicity, could picture it this way. According to this conception, God might have said, "Son, I hate to see you go. I sure am going to miss you. I love you with all my heart. But I do want you to go down to earth and tell those poor souls down there how to live and point them to the way that will lead them back home."

Sam said he thought that the last thing God said to Jesus was, "Give them all my love." Now that's simple—but it's human and divine.

So when the carols and the Bible reading ended and we walked back to the eating tent for our dinner, I knew with a complete sense of peace that where Christmas is concerned, surroundings do not matter, because the spirit of Jesus is everywhere, knocking on the doors of our hearts, asking to be taken in.

The festive lights and the gifts and the ornaments are fine, but they are only a setting for the real jewel: the birth of a Baby that marked the descent of God himself to mankind. That's where the true meaning of Christmas lies. And it can be found in that simple sentence: "Give them all my love."

—Norman Vincent Peale

'TWAS THE NIGHT BEFORE CHRISTMAS

'Twas the night before Christmas,
When all through the house,
Not a creature was stirring,
not even a mouse.

The stockings were hung
by the chimney with care,
In hopes that St. Nicholas
soon would be there;

The children were nestled all snug in their beds;
While visions of sugarplums danced in their heads;

Momma in her 'kerchief and I in my cap,
Had just settled down for a long winter's nap,—

When out on the lawn there arose such a clatter,
I sprang from my bed to see what was the matter;

Away to the window, I flew like a flash,
Tore open the shutters and threw up the sash.

The moon on the breast of the new-fallen snow
Gave a luster of midday to objects below;

When, what to my wondering eyes should appear,
But a miniature sleigh and eight tiny reindeer;

With a little old driver so lively and quick,
I knew in a moment it must be St. Nick.

More rapid than eagles his coursers they came,
And he whistled, and shouted, and called them by name.

"Now, Dasher! now, Dancer! Now, Prancer and Vixen!
On Comet! on Cupid! On, Donder and Blitzen!

To the top of the porch! To the top of the wall!
Now dash away! dash away! dash away all!"

As dry leaves that before the wild hurricane fly,
When they meet with an obstacle, mount to the sky,

So up to the house-top the coursers, they flew.
With a sleigh full of toys—and St. Nicholas, too!

And then in a twinkling, I heard on the roof,
The prancing and pawing of each little hoof.

As I drew in my head, and was turning around,
Down the chimney St. Nicholas came with a bound.

He was dressed all in fur, from his head to his foot,
And his clothes were all tarnished with ashes and soot!

A bundle of toys he had flung on his back,
And he looked like a peddler just opening his pack;

His eyes—how they twinkled! his dimples, how merry!
His cheeks were like roses, his nose like a cherry!

His droll little mouth was drawn up like a bow,
And the beard on his chin was as white as the snow.

The stump of his pipe he held tight in his teeth,
And the smoke, it encircled his head like a wreath.

He had a broad face, and a little round belly,
That shook when he laugh'd like a bowl full of jelly.

He was chubby and plump; a right jolly old elf;
And I laughed when I saw him, in spite of myself.

A wink of his eye, and a twist of his head,
Soon gave me to know I had nothing to dread.

He spoke not a word, but went straight to his work,
And filled all the stockings—then turned with a jerk,

And laying his finger aside his nose,
And giving a nod, up the chimney he rose.

He sprang to his sleigh, to his team gave a whistle,
And away they all flew, like the down of a thistle.

But I heard him exclaim, 'ere he drove out of sight,
"Merry Christmas to all! and to all a good-night!"

           —Clement C. Moore

Household Angels

In the rush of early morning,
When the red burns through the gray,
And the wintry world lies waiting
For the glory of the day.
Then we hear a fitful rustling
Just without upon the stair,
See two small white phantoms coming,
Catch the gleam of sunny hair.

Are they Christmas fairies stealing
Rows of little socks to fill?
Are they angels floating hither
With their message of good-will?
What sweet spell are these elves weaving,
As like larks they chirp and sing?
Are these palms of peace from heaven
That these lovely spirits bring?

Rosy feet upon the threshold,
Eager faces peeping through,
With the first red ray of sunshine,
Chanting cherubs come in view;
Mistletoe and gleaming holly,
Symbols of a blessed day,
In their chubby hands they carry,
Streaming all along the way.

Well we know them,
Never weary
Of this innocent surprise;
Waiting, watching, listening always
With full hearts and tender eyes,
While our little household angels,
White and golden in the sun,
Greet us with the sweet old welcome—
"Merry Christmas, every one!"

—Louisa May Alcott—

MERRY CHRISTMAS

M for the Music, merry and clear;
E for the Eve, the crown of the year;
R for the Romping of bright girls and boys;
R for the Reindeer that bring them the toys;
Y for the Yule log softly aglow.

C for the Cold of the sky and the snow;
H for the Hearth where they hang up the hose;
R for the Reel which the old folks propose;
I for the Icicles seen through the pane;
S for the Sleigh bells, with tinkling refrain;
T for the Tree with gifts all abloom;
M for the Mistletoe hung in the room;
A for the Anthems we all love to hear;
S is for St. Nicholas—joy of the year!

—From St. Nicholas Magazine
January 1897

YES, VIRGINIA, THERE IS A SANTA CLAUS.

We take pleasure in answering at once and thus prominently, the communication below, expressing at the same time our great gratification that its faithful author is numbered among the friends of The Sun:

September 21, 1897

Dear Editor:

I am 8 years old. Some of my little friends say there is no Santa Claus. Papa says 'If you see it in The Sun *it's so.' Please tell me the truth, is there a Santa Claus?*

Virginia O'Hanlon

115 W. 95th Street

Virginia, your little friends are wrong. They have been affected by the skepticism of a skeptical age. They do not believe except they see. They think that nothing can be which is not comprehensible by their little minds. All minds, Virginia, whether they be men's or children's, are little. In this great universe of ours man is a mere insect, an ant in his intellect, as compared with the boundless world about him, as measured by the intelligence capable of grasping the whole of truth and knowledge.

Yes, Virginia, there is a Santa Claus. He exists as certainly as love and generosity and devotion exist, and you know that they abound and give to your life its highest beauty and joy. Alas! How dreary would be the world if there were no Santa Claus! It would be as dreary as if there were no Virginias. There would be no childlike faith then, no poetry, no romance to make tolerable this existence. We should have no enjoyment, except in sense and sight. The eternal light with which childhood fills the world would be extinguished.

Not believe in Santa Claus! You might as well not believe in fairies! You might get your papa to hire men to watch in all the chimneys on Christmas Eve to catch Santa Claus; but even if they did not see Santa Claus coming down, what would that prove? Nobody sees Santa Claus, but that is no sign that there is no Santa Claus. The most real things in the world are those that neither children nor men can see. Did you ever see fairies dancing on the lawn? Of course not, but that's no proof that they are not there. Nobody can conceive or imagine all the wonders there are unseen and unseeable in the world.

You can tear apart the baby's rattle and see what makes the noise inside, but there is a veil covering the unseen world which not the strongest men that ever lived could tear apart. Only faith, fancy, poetry, love, romance, can push aside that curtain and view and picture the supernal beauty and glory beyond. Is it all real? Ah, Virginia, in all this world there is nothing else real and abiding.

No Santa Claus! Thank God he lives, and he lives forever. A thousand years from now, Virginia, nay ten thousand years from now, he will continue to make glad the heart of childhood.

—Francis Pharcellus Church, 1897

*May the fire of this log warm the cold;
may the hungry be fed;
may the weary find rest,
and may all enjoy Heaven's peace.*

—Yule log prayer—

A Santa Suit Does Not a Santa Claus Make

Each time the pressures of a Christmas season begin to get to me, and one more piped-in carol assaults my ears in yet another crowded shopping mall, I think of a Christmas so many years ago when I was a very young teacher. The school was alive with activity as we prepared for the special days to come. There was much to do. We had to decorate our classrooms, rehearse our parts in the Christmas play, plan the trip to sing in a local retirement home, and, of course, make the much-anticipated gifts for Mom and Dad.

One day prior to the holiday break, I was called to the principal's office. Our usually calm and collected principal seemed to be in a state of high anxiety. "We've lost our Santa Claus!" she moaned. "Mr. Ruggles is usually our Santa, but he is ill. A very bad cold, maybe even pneumonia."

I couldn't imagine Mr. Ruggles, the school custodian, being ill. He was a large, jovial man with a bright sunny face and rosy cheeks that would be the envy of any Santa Claus.

I was beginning to recover from the news when I heard the principal suggest that since I was the only other man in the school (male teachers in elementary schools were rare at that time), I was the logical replacement. She explained that she herself had considered replacing him, but a woman Santa just wouldn't do.

"I know you'll do it," she said. "You would never disappoint the children."

The idea sounded like madness to me. In the first place, I was so thin at the time that I was compelled to buy my clothes in children's sizes. And though I could manage a booming voice when necessary, I knew I wasn't up to the traditional "Ho, ho, ho!"—so important to an authentic Santa Claus.

"But I don't look anything like Santa Claus. The kids will see it in a minute and laugh me out of the room," I protested.

"Nonsense," she assured me, "you'll make a magnificent Santa. It's nothing. All you have to do is visit each classroom with the bag of toys. When you see the children, greet them and be merry, pass out candy canes, then make a fast exit to your next room. I'll carry the bells."

"But..." I tried to interject, though I could see that it was useless. She was already

dragging me into her office, where she had a large Santa outfit draped across her desk.

"Now get into this quickly,"she said.

"But what about my classroom?" I made one last effort.

"Never mind. We'll get it covered."

"But I'll make a miserable Santa."

"Well, even a miserable Santa will be better than none at all," she replied, and left me to change clothes.

In a few minutes she was back, stuffing pillows inside the Santa suit, fitting the cap on my head over the white wig, gluing on the beard and painting bright rosy cheeks and lips on my face. When she was finished, I looked in the mirror and was pleasantly surprised to discover that I actually made a respectable-looking Santa.

"Come on, now," the principal encouraged me. "Let's have a big Christmas smile!" I found that a little difficult to accomplish, but I managed a little grin.

I tightened the black belt around my billowing pillows and followed her jingling bells out into the hall. "We'll go to the kindergarten first," she told me as we approached Room 1.

The response to my entrance was deafening. Sounds of clapping hands and screams of delight filled the room. With glowing eyes and grasping hands, the children surrounded me, attaching themselves to my spindly legs and very nearly pulling my oversized pants down around my ankles.

"Ho, ho, ho," I heard myself say, not being able to think of anything more creative. "Have you all been good boys and girls?"

"Y-E-E-E-E-S!" came the joyous response.

"Not John," said one of the more poised girls, in a rather motherly tone of voice. "He hasn't been good, has he, teacher?"

"Well," stammered the teacher, rather stunned, "he's trying."

"I have candy for everyone," I said. In an instant I was downed like a quarterback in a failed play, inundated with tiny bodies bursting with anticipation.

With a firm voice, the teacher saved me from suffocation. I quickly regained my lost dignity and took the occasion to hand out the candy canes to the eager extended hands. I had never seen such happy faces, such unaffected joy. It didn't matter to them that by this time I had become totally unglued, my mustache hanging precariously over my lips,

my gigantic stomach sliding down over my legs. None of these things mattered to the children. I was Santa Claus, and that was all that had any real importance. This joy-filled spirit was evident in each classroom, no matter the children's ages.

Though I had felt awkward and tentative at the start, I was soon caught up in the wonder of what was happening. I found myself behaving like the kind old man himself, the giver of good things, the renewer of hope, the dispenser of magic. For a while I was certain that I could actually make dreams into realities, turn the mundane into wonder.

For the first time I realized how powerful the symbol of Santa is. With a "Ho, ho, ho" he has the power to paint a drab classroom the color of sunshine, and turn an often cheerless school into a wonderland.

When I returned to the principal's office, fifteen classrooms later, I was in a pretty ragged state. I removed my costume and makeup. The principal and teachers streamed in and out to offer congratulations on my stunning performance and to assure me that I had saved Christmas.

Most of the cars were gone when I went to the school parking lot later that afternoon. I had left Santa Claus where I had found him, draped over the principal's desk. As I was about to open the door of my car, I saw one of the children coming toward me, devouring the candy cane Santa had given him.

"How did you like Santa Claus?" I asked him.

"Oh," he answered. "You were great, Mr. B."

I was stunned. So the children had recognized me all along, yet it hadn't mattered. They hadn't expected the real Santa Claus; any symbol was fine with them—even a rather ragged, skinny one.

Now during the Christmas season, when I find myself trying to deal with the pressures of the time and all the trappings of a commercialized Christmas, I stop and recall what the children taught me on that special day. It isn't the Santa suit that makes the Santa, any more than it is the tinsel, colored lights, and sound of cash registers that make Christmas. Then, like a child, I gather my gifts and, savoring a candy cane, I start for home, renewed and ready for the celebration and the true wonder that is uniquely Christmas.

—Leo Buscaglia

FRANCIE NOLAN'S CHRISTMAS TREE

Christmas was a charmed time in Brooklyn in 1912. The spruce trees began coming into Francie Nolan's neighborhood the week before Christmas. Their branches were corded to make shipping easier. Vendors rented space on the curb before a store and stretched a rope from pole to pole and leaned the trees against it. All day they walked up and down this one-sided avenue of aromatic leaning trees, blowing on stiff ungloved fingers. And the air was cold and stiff, and full of the pine smell and the smell of tangerines which appeared in the stores only at Christmastime and the mean street was truly wonderful for awhile.

There was a cruel custom in the neighborhood. At midnight on the Eve of our dear Saviour's birth, the kids gathered where there were unsold trees. There was a saying that if you waited until then, you wouldn't have to buy a tree; that "they'd chuck 'em at you." This was literally true. The man threw each tree in turn, starting with the biggest. Kids volunteered to stand up against the throwing. If a boy didn't fall down under the impact, the tree was his. If he fell, he forfeited his chance at winning a tree. Only the roughest boys and some of the young men elected to be hit by the big trees. The others waited shrewdly until a tree came up that they could stand against. The littlest kids waited for the tiny, foot-high trees and shrieked in delight when they won one.

On the Christmas Eve when Francie was ten and her brother, Neely, nine, Mama consented to let them go down and have their first try for a tree. Francie had picked out her tree earlier in the day. She had stood near it all afternoon and evening praying that no one would buy it. To her joy, it was still there at midnight. It was ten feet tall and its price was so high that no one could afford to buy it. Its branches were bound with new white rope and it came to a sure pure point at the top.

The man took this tree out first. Before Francie could speak up, a neighborhood bully, a boy of eighteen known as Punky Perkins, stepped forward and ordered the

man to chuck the tree at him. The man hated the way Punky was so confident. He looked around and asked, "Anybody else wanna take a chance on it?"

Francie stepped forward, "Me, mister."

A spurt of derisive laughter came from the tree man. The kids snickered. A few adults who had gathered to watch the fun guffawed. "Aw g'wan. You're too little," the tree man objected.

"Me and my brother—we're not too little together."

She pulled Neely forward. The man looked at them—a thin little girl of ten with starveling hollows in her cheeks but with the chin still baby-round. He looked at the little boy with his fair hair and round blue eyes—Neely Nolan, all innocence and trust.

"Two ain't fair," yelped Punky.

"Shut your lousy trap," advised the man, who held all the power in that hour. "These here kids is got nerve. Stand back, the rest of you'se. These kids is goin' to have a show at this tree."

The others made a wavering lane, a human funnel with Francie and her brother making the small end of it. The big man at the other end flexed his great arms to throw the great tree. He noticed how tiny the children looked at the end of the short lane. For a split part of a moment, the tree thrower went through a kind of Gethsemane.

Oh, his soul agonized, *why don't I just give 'em the tree and say Merry Christmas? I can't sell it no more this year and it won't keep till next year.* The kids watched him solemnly as he stood there in his moment of thought. *But then,* he rationalized, *if I did that, all the others would expect to get 'em handed to 'em. And next year, nobody a-tall would buy a tree off of me. I ain't a big enough man to give this tree away for nothin'. No, I gotta think of myself and my own kids.* He finally came to his conclusion. *Them two kids is gotta live in this world. They got to learn to give and take punishment.* As he threw the tree with all his strength, his heart wailed out, *It's a rotten, lousy world!*

Francie saw the tree leave his hands. The whole world stood still as something dark and monstrous came through the air. There was nothing but pungent darkness and something that grew and grew as it rushed at her. She staggered as the tree hit

them. Neely went to his knees but she pulled him up fiercely before he could go down. There was a mighty swishing sound as the tree settled. Everything was dark, green and prickly. Then she felt a sharp pain at the side of her head where the trunk of the tree had hit her. She felt Neely trembling.

When some of the older boys pulled the tree away, they found Francie and her brother standing upright, hand in hand. Blood was coming from scratches on Neely's face. He looked more like a baby than ever with his bewildered blue eyes, and the fairness of his skin made more noticeable because of the clear red blood. But they were smiling. Had they not won the biggest tree in the neighborhood? Some of the boys hollered, "Hooray!" A few adults clapped. The tree man eulogized them by screaming, "And now get out of here with your tree!"

Such phrases could mean many things according to the tone used in saying them. So Francie smiled tremulously at the kind man. She knew that he was really saying, "Goodbye—God bless you."

It wasn't easy dragging that tree home. They were handicapped by a boy who ran alongside yelping, "Free ride! All aboard!" who'd jump on and make them drag him along. But he got sick of the game eventually and went away.

In a way, it was good that it took them so long to get the tree home. It made their triumph more drawn out. Francie glowed when a lady said, "I never saw such a big tree!" The cop on their corner stopped them, examined the tree, and solemnly offered to buy it for fifteen cents if they'd deliver it to his home. Francie nearly burst with pride although she knew he was joking.

They had to call Papa to help them get the tree up the narrow stairs. Papa came running down. His amazement at the size of the tree was flattering. He pretended to believe that it wasn't theirs. Francie had a lot of fun convincing him although she knew all the while that the whole thing was make-believe. Papa pulled in front and Francie and Neely pushed in back and they began forcing the big tree up the two narrow flights of stairs. Papa started singing, not caring that it was rather late at night. He sang *"O, Holy Night."* The narrow walls took up his clear sweet voice, held it for a breath and gave it back with doubled sweetness. Doors creaked open and families gathered on the landings, pleased

and amazed at something unexpected being added to that moment of their lives.

Francie saw the Tynmore sisters, who gave piano lessons, standing together in their doorway, their gray hair in crimpers, and ruffled, starched nightgowns showing under their voluminous wrappers. They added their thin poignant voices to Papa's. Flossie Gladis, her mother and her brother Henny, who was dying of consumption, stood in their doorway. Henny was crying and when Papa saw him he let the song trail off; he thought maybe it made Henny too sad.

Flossie was in a Klondike-dance-hall-girl costume waiting for an escort to take her to a masquerade ball which started soon after midnight. More to make Henny smile than anything else, Papa said, "Floss, we got no angel for the top of this Christmas tree, how about you obliging?"

Flossie was all ready to make a smart-alecky reply, but there was something about the big proud tree, the beaming children and the rare goodwill of the neighbors that changed her mind. All she said was, "Gee, ain't you the kidder, Mr. Nolan."

They set the tree up in the front room after Mama had spread a sheet to protect the carpet from falling pine needles. The tree stood in a big tin bucket with broken bricks to hold it upright. When the rope was cut away, the branches spread out to fill the room. They draped over the piano and some of the chairs stood among the branches. There was no money to buy decorations or lights. But the great tree standing there was enough. The room was cold. It was a poor year, that one—too poor for them to buy the extra coal for the front room stove. The room smelled cold, clean and aromatic.

Every day, during the week the tree stood there, Francie put on her sweater and stocking cap and went in and sat under the tree. She sat there and enjoyed the smell and the dark greenness of it.

Oh, the mystery of a great tree, a prisoner in a tin wash bucket in a tenement front room!

—Betty Smith

THE LITTLE BLUE DISHES

Once upon a time there was a poor woodcutter who lived with his wife and three children in Germany. There was a big boy called Hans, a little boy named Peterkin and a little sister named Gretchen, just five years old. When Christmas was getting near, the children went to the toy shop to look at all the toys.

"Gretchen," said Peterkin, "what do you like best?"

"Oh! That little box of blue dishes," said Gretchen. "That is the very best of all."

On Christmas Eve they hung up their stockings, although their mother had said that they would not have much this Christmas. Hans ran out after supper to play. Gretchen and Peterkin sat talking about Christmas toys and especially about the box of blue dishes. After Gretchen ran off to bed, Peterkin looked in his bank. There was only one penny, but he took it and ran to the toy shop.

"What have you for a penny?" he said to the toy man.

"Only a small candy heart with a picture on it," said the man.

"But I want that set of blue dishes," said Peterkin.

"Oh, they cost ten cents," said the man.

So Peterkin bought the candy heart and put it in Gretchen's stocking, and then he ran off to bed.

Soon, Hans came home, cold and hungry. When he saw Gretchen's stocking he peeked in, then put his hand in and drew out the candy heart. "Oh," said Hans, "how good this smells," and before he knew it, he had eaten it. "Oh, no, that was for Gretchen. I'll go buy something else for her." He found ten pennies in his bank then he ran to the toy store.

"What have you got for ten pennies?" he asked the storekeeper.

"I'm almost sold out," said the toy man, "but here is this little set of blue dishes."

"I will take them," said Hans, and home he ran to drop the dishes into Gretchen's stocking. Then he went to bed.

Early in the morning the children came running downstairs.

"Oh!" said Gretchen. "Look at my stocking!" And when she saw the blue dishes, she was as happy as could be. But Peterkin could never understand how his candy heart had changed into a box of blue dishes.

—Anonymous

 37

THE CHRISTMAS MIRACLE

On the morning before the Christmas that fell when I was six, my father took my brother and me for a walk in the woods of the Old Colony town where we lived. Three times as we walked he stopped, and cut a small balsam tree. There was a very tiny one, hardly more than a seedling; a small one a foot or so high; and a youthful one of perhaps four feet. So we each had a tree to bear, flaglike, back to the house. It didn't occur to us single-minded larvae that this had the least connection with Christmas. Our father was a botanist Ph.D., given to plucking all manner of specimens whenever we walked, with the offhand explanation, "A fine Tsuga canadensis," or whatever it was. By nightfall we had forgotten all about our walk.

For this was Christmas Eve, and we were suddenly in a panic. Where was The Tree? From experience, we knew that it was usually delivered in the morning, that Father set it up in the afternoon and that Mother trimmed it at night, letting us help with the ornaments before she put us to bed in a fever of anticipation. But this year we had seen no tree arrive; look where we would, we could not find one; and even Mother turned aside our questions. Would there be no Tree? Would there, perhaps, be no Christmas at all for us? How we wished now, that we had not put the cat in the milk-pail!

But after supper Father and Mother took us into the sitting-room. In a cleared corner by the big closet stood a jar of earth. "Christmas," said Father, "is a day of miracles, to remind us of the greatest Miracle of all. Perhaps we shall see one." Then Mother led us out, closing the door on Father and the jar of earth—and the closet.

"We can help," she said, "by learning this song." And she began, softly but very true. *"O Little Town of Bethlehem."* We tried hard in our shrill way. But even Mother had to admit it was only a good try. Yet when the door opened and we went again into the sitting-room, behold! A tiny Tree had appeared in the jar of earth! Hardly more than a seedling, to be sure, and not old enough yet to bear ornaments, but indubitably a Tree. Marveling, we went out again.

This time we did better—on the words if not the tune. And when we re-entered the sitting room, the Tree had grown—to perhaps a foot or so in height! A blaze of hope flashed upon us. We went out and tried harder on that song. And sure enough,

this time the Tree was taller than either boy. Terrific! We could hardly wait to get outside and sing some more with Mother. For now hope was a rapture of certainty.

To this day I cannot hear *"O Little Town of Bethlehem,"* from however cracked a curbside organ, without hearing through and beyond it the clear, true voice of my mother. Nor hear that long-vanished sweetness without knowing that presently, somewhere, somehow a great door is going to open and disclose unearthly beauty. It is more than sixty years since our sitting-room door swung back for the fourth time, that night in the Old Colony of Massachusetts. But I can still see, sharp as life, the splendor of the Tree that towered to the ceiling in its glossy dark green, sparkling with silver tinsel, glowing with candles and half hiding in its crisp, fragrant needles, the incomparable perfection of spheres that shone like far-off other worlds, red and blue and green and gold.

Cynics say that miracles are all man made—contrived, like a Christmas tree hidden in a closet and flashed upon wondering kids.   That even the Christmas spirit is only a spell we work up to bemuse one another—and then fall for, ourselves, like so many simple children. What of it? So much the better! If mankind, by its own devoted labor, can induce in itself—if only for a day—an all-pervading spirit of friendship and cheer and good will and loving kindness, that alone is a very great miracle. It is the kind of miracle that must please above all others Him who knows how miracles are wrought.

—Robert Keith Leavitt

CHRISTMAS DAY IN THE MORNING

He waked suddenly and completely. It was four o'clock, the hour at which his father had always called him to get up and help with the milking. Strange how the habits of his youth clung to him still! Fifty years ago, and his father had been dead for thirty years, and yet he waked at four o'clock in the morning. He had trained himself to turn over and go to sleep, but this morning, because it was Christmas, he did not try to sleep.

Yet what was the magic of Christmas now? His childhood and youth were long past, and his own children had grown up and gone. Some of them lived only a few miles away but they had their own families, and though they would come in as usual toward the end of the day, they had explained with infinite gentleness that they wanted their children to build Christmas memories about *their* houses, not his. He was left alone with his wife.

Yesterday she had said, "It isn't worth while, perhaps—"

And he had said, "Oh, yes, Alice, even if there are only the two of us, let's have a Christmas tree of our own."

Then she had said, "Let's not trim the tree until tomorrow, Robert—just so it's ready when the children come. I'm tired."

He had agreed, and the tree was still out in the back entry.

He lay in his bed in the big room. The door to her room was shut because she was a light sleeper, and sometimes he had restless nights. Years ago they had decided to use separate rooms. It meant nothing, they said, except that neither of them slept as well as they once had. They had been married so long that nothing could separate them, actually.

Why did he feel so awake tonight? For it was a still night, a clear and starry night. No moon, of course, but the stars were extraordinary! Now that he thought of it, the

stars seemed always large and clear before the dawn of Christmas Day. There was one star now that was certainly larger and brighter than any of the others. He could even imagine it moving, as it had seemed to him to move one night long ago. He slipped back in time, as he did so easily nowadays.

*   *   *   *   *   *   *   *   *   *

He was fifteen years old and still on his father's farm. He loved his father. He had not known it until one day a few days before Christmas when he overheard what his father was saying to his mother.

"Mary, I hate to call Rob in the mornings. He's growing so fast, and he needs his sleep. If you could see how he sleeps when I go in to wake him up! I wish I could manage alone."

"Well, you can't, Adam." His mother's voice was brisk. "Besides, he isn't a child anymore. It's time he took his turn."

"Yes," his father said slowly. "But I sure do hate to wake him."

When he heard these words, something in him woke: his father loved him! He had never thought of it before, taking for granted the tie of their blood. Neither his father nor his mother talked about loving their children—they had no time for such things. There was always so much to do on a farm.

Now that he knew that his father loved him, there would be no more loitering in the mornings and having to be called again. He got up after that, stumbling with sleep, and pulled on his clothes, his eyes tight shut, but he got up.

And then on the night before Christmas, that year when he was fifteen, he lay for a few minutes thinking about the next day. They were poor, and most of the excitement was in the turkey they had raised themselves and in the mince pies his mother made. His sisters sewed presents and his mother and father always bought something he needed, not only a warm jacket, maybe, but something more, such as a book. And he saved and bought them each something, too.

He wished, that Christmas, when he was fifteen, he had a better present for his father. As usual, he had gone to the ten-cent store and bought a tie. It had seemed nice enough until he lay thinking the night before Christmas, and then he wished that he had heard his father and mother talking in time for him to save for something better.

He lay on his side, his head supported by his elbow, and looked out of his attic window. The stars were bright, much brighter than he ever remembered seeing them, and one was so bright he wondered if it were really the star of Bethlehem.

"Dad," he had once asked when he was a little boy, "what is a stable?"

"It's just a barn," his father had replied, "like ours."

Jesus had been born in a barn, and to a barn the shepherds and the Wise Men had come, bringing their Christmas gifts!

The thought struck him like a silver dagger. Why should he not give his father a special gift, too, out there in the barn? He could get up early, earlier than four o'clock, and he could creep into the barn and get all the milking done. He'd do it alone, milk and clean up, and then when his father went in to start the milking, he'd see it all done. And he would know who had done it.

At a quarter to three, he got up and put on his clothes. He crept downstairs, careful of the creaky boards, and let himself out. The big star hung lower over the barn, a reddish-gold. The cows looked at him, sleepy and surprised.

"So, boss," he whispered. They accepted him placidly, and he fetched some hay for each cow and then got the milking pail and the big milk cans.

He had never milked all alone before, but it seemed almost easy. He kept thinking about his father's surprise. His father would come in and call him, saying that he would get things started while Rob was getting dressed. He'd go to the barn, open the door, and then he'd go to get the two big empty milk cans. But they wouldn't be empty; they'd be standing in the milk house, filled.

The task went more easily than he had ever known it to before. Milking for once was not a chore. It was something else, a gift to his father who loved him. He finished, the two milk cans were full, and he covered them and closed the milk-house door carefully, making sure of the latch. He put the stool in its place by the door and hung up the clean milk pail. Then he went out of the barn and barred the door behind him.

Back in his room, he had only a minute to pull off his clothes in the darkness and jump into bed, for he heard his father up. He put the covers over his head to silence his quick breathing.

The door opened.

"Rob!" his father called. "We have to get up, Son, even if it is Christmas."

"Aw-right," he said sleepily.

"I'll go on out," his father said. "I'll get things started."

The door closed and he lay still, laughing to himself. In just a few minutes his father would know. His dancing heart was ready to jump from his body.

The minutes were endless—ten, fifteen, he did not know how many—and he heard his father's footsteps again. The door opened and he lay still.

"Rob!"

"Yes, Dad—"

His father was laughing, a queer sobbing sort of laugh.

"Thought you'd fooled me, did you?" His father was standing beside his bed, feeling for him, pulling away the cover.

"It's for Christmas, Dad!"

He found his father and clutched him in a great hug. He felt his father's arms go around him. It was dark, and they could not see each other's faces.

"Son, I thank you. Nobody ever did a nicer thing—"

"Oh, Dad, I want you to know—I do want to be good!" The words broke from him of their own will. He did not know what to say. His heart was bursting with love.

"Well, I reckon I can go back to bed and sleep," his father said after a moment. "No, hark—the little ones are waked up. Come to think of it, Son, I've never seen you children when you first saw the Christmas tree. I was always in the barn. Come on!"

He got up and he pulled on his clothes again, and they went down to the Christmas tree and soon the sun was creeping up to where the star had been. Oh, what a Christmas, and how his heart had nearly burst again with shyness and pride as his father told his mother and made the younger children listen about how he, Rob, had got up all by himself.

"The best Christmas gift I ever had, and I'll remember it Son, every year on Christmas morning, so long as I live."

They had both remembered it, and now that his father was dead he remembered

it alone: that blessed Christmas dawn when, alone with the cows in the barn, he had made his first gift of true love.

*   *   *   *   *   *   *   *   *   *

Outside the window now the great star slowly sank. He got up out of bed and put on his slippers and bathrobe and went softly upstairs to the attic and found the box of Christmas decorations. He took them downstairs into the living room. Then he brought in the tree. It was a little one—they had not had a big tree since the children went away—but he set it in the holder and put it in the middle of the long table under the window. Then carefully he began to trim it.

It was done very soon, the time passing as quickly as it had that morning long ago in the barn. He went to his library and fetched the little box that contained his special gift to his wife, a star of diamonds, not large but dainty in design. He had written the card for it the day before. He tied the gift on the tree and then stood back. It was pretty, very pretty and she would be surprised.

But he was not satisfied. He wanted to tell her—to tell her how much he loved her. It had been a long time since he had really told her, although he loved her in a very special way, much more than he ever had when they were young.

He had been fortunate that she had loved him—and how fortunate that he had been able to love! Ah, that was the true joy of life, the ability to love! For he was quite sure that some people were genuinely unable to love anyone. But love was alive in him, it still was.

It occurred to him suddenly that it was alive because long ago it had been born in him when he knew his father loved him. That was it: love alone would awaken love.

And he could give the gift again and again. This morning, this blessed Christmas morning, he would give it to his beloved wife. He could write it down in a letter for her to read and keep forever. He went to his desk and began his love letter to his wife: *My dearest love...*

When it was finished he sealed it and tied it on the tree where she could see it the first thing when she came into the room. She would read it, surprised and then moved, and realize how very much he loved her.

He put out the light and went tiptoeing up the stairs. The stars in the sky were gone, and the first rays of the sun were gleaming the sky. Such a happy, happy Christmas!

—Pearl S. Buck

THE GIFT OF THE MAGI

One dollar and eighty-seven cents. That was all. And sixty cents of it was in pennies. Three times Della counted it. One dollar and eighty-seven cents. And the next day would be Christmas.

There was clearly nothing to do but flop down on the shabby little couch and howl. So Della did it.

In the vestibule below was a letter-box into which no letter would go, and an electric button from which no mortal finger could coax a ring. There was a card bearing the name "Mr. James Dillingham Young."

Della finished her cry and attended to her cheeks with a powder rag. She stood by the window and looked out dully at the gray cat walking a grey fence in a gray backyard. Tomorrow would be Christmas Day, and she had only $1.87 with which to buy Jim a present. She had been saving every penny she could for months, with this result. Twenty dollars a week doesn't go far. Expenses had been greater than she had calculated. They always are. Only $1.87 to buy a present for Jim. Her Jim. Many a happy hour she had spent planning for something nice for him. Something fine and rare and sterling—something worthy of Jim.

Suddenly she whirled from the window and stood before the mirror. Her eyes were shining brilliantly, but her face had lost its color within twenty seconds. Rapidly she pulled down her hair and let it fall to its full length.

Now, there were two possessions of the James Dillingham Young's in which they both took a mighty pride. One was Jim's gold watch which had been his father's and grandfather's. The other was Della's hair. Had the Queen of Sheba lived in the flat across the airshaft, Della would have let her hair hang out the window some day to dry just to depreciate Her Majesty's jewels and gifts. Had King Solomon been the janitor, with all his treasures piled up in the basement, Jim would have pulled out his watch every time he passed, just to see him pluck at his beard from envy.

So now Della's beautiful hair fell about her rippling and shining like a cascade of brown waters. It reached below her knee and made itself almost like a garment for her.

On went her old brown jacket; on went her old brown hat. With a whirl of skirts

and with the brilliant sparkle still in her eyes, she fluttered out the door and down the stairs to the street.

Where she stopped the sign read: "Mme. Sofronie. Hair. Goods of all Kinds." One flight up Della ran, and collected herself, panting.

"Will you buy my hair?" asked Della.

"I buy hair," said Madame. "Take ye hat off and let's have a sight at the looks of it."

Down rippled the brown cascade.

"Twenty dollars," said Madame, lifting the mass with a practiced hand.

"Give it to me quick," said Della.

The next two hours tripped by on rosy wings. Della was ransacking the stores for Jim's present.

She found it at last. It surely had been made for Jim and no one else. There was no other like it in any of the stores, and she had turned all of them inside out. It was a platinum fob chain, simple and chaste in design. It was worthy of The Watch. As soon as she saw it she knew that it must be Jim's. It was like him. Quietness and value—the description applied to both. Twenty-one dollars they took from her for it, and she hurried home with the 87 cents.

When Della reached home her intoxication gave way a little to prudence and reason. She got out her curling irons and went to work repairing the ravages. Within forty minutes her head was covered with tiny, close-lying curls that made her look wonderfully like a truant schoolboy. She looked at her reflection in the mirror, long, carefully and critically.

"If Jim doesn't kill me," she said to herself, "before he takes a second look at me, he'll say I look like a Coney Island chorus girl. But what could I do—oh! what could I do with a dollar and eighty-seven cents?"

At 7 o'clock the coffee was made and the frying pan was on the back of the stove, hot and ready to cook the chops for dinner. Jim was never late. Della doubled the fob chain in her hand and sat on the corner of the table near the door that he always entered. Then she heard his step on the stairway down on the first flight, and she turned white for just a moment. She had a habit of saying little silent prayers about the simplest everyday things, and now she whispered: "Please God, make him think I am still pretty."

The door opened and Jim stepped in and closed it. He looked thin and very serious. Poor fellow, he was only twenty-two. He needed a new overcoat and he was without gloves.

Jim stopped inside the door. His eyes were fixed upon Della, and there was an expression in them that she could not read, and it terrified her. It was not anger, nor surprise, nor disapproval, nor horror. He simply stared at her fixedly with that peculiar expression on his face. Della wriggled off the table and went to him.

"Jim, darling," she cried, "don't look at me that way. I had my hair cut off and sold it because I couldn't have lived through Christmas without giving you a present. It'll grow out again—you won't mind will you? I just had to do it. My hair grows awfully fast. Say 'Merry Christmas!' Jim, and let's be happy. You don't know what a nice—what a beautiful nice gift I've got for you."

"You've cut off your hair?" asked Jim.

"Cut if off and sold it," said Della. "Don't you like me just as well, anyhow? I'm me without my hair, ain't I?"

Jim looked about the room curiously. "You say your hair is gone?" he said, with an air almost of idiocy. Then Jim drew a package from his overcoat pocket and threw it upon the table.

"Don't make any mistake, Dell," he said. "I don't think there's anything in the way of a haircut or a shave or a shampoo that could make me like my girl any less. But if you'll unwrap that package you may see why you had me going a while at first."

White fingers tore at the string and paper. And then an ecstatic scream of joy; and then, alas! a quick change to hysterical tears, for there lay The Combs—the set of combs, side and back, that Della had worshiped for so long in a Broadway window. Beautiful combs, pure tortoise shell, with jewelled rims—just the shade to wear in her beautiful but vanished hair. They were expensive combs, she knew, and her heart had simply craved and yearned over them without the least hope of possession. And now, they were hers, but the tresses that should have adorned the coveted adornments were gone. But she hugged them to her bosom, and at length she was able to look up with dim eyes and a smile and say: "My hair grows so fast Jim!"

Jim had not yet seen his beautiful present. She held it out to him eagerly upon her open palm. "Isn't it a dandy, Jim? I hunted all over town to find it. Give me your watch. I want to see how it looks on it."

Jim tumbled down on the couch and put his hands under the back of his head and smiled. "Dell," said he, "let's put our Christmas presents away and keep 'em a while. I sold the watch to get the money to buy your combs. And now, suppose you put the chops on . . ."

The Magi, as you know, were wise men—wonderfully wise men—who brought gifts to the Babe in the manger. They invented the art of giving Christmas presents. Being wise, their gifts were no doubt wise ones.

Here, I have related to you a chronicle of two children who sacrificed for each other the greatest treasures of their house. But let it be said that of all who give gifts, these two were the wisest. Of all who give and receive gifts, such as they are wisest. Everywhere they are wisest. They are the Magi.

—O'Henry

KEEPING CHRISTMAS

In a world that seems not only to be changing,

but even to be dissolving,

there are some tens of millions of us

who want Christmas to be the same…

with the same old "Merry Christmas" and no other.

We long for the abiding love among men of good will

which the season brings…

believing in this ancient miracle of Christmas with its softening,

sweetening influence to tug at our heart strings once again.

We want to hold on to the old customs and traditions

because they strengthen our family ties,

bind us to our friends,

make us one with all mankind

for whom the Child was born,

and bring us back again to the God

Who gave His only begotten Son,

that "whosoever believeth *in Him should not perish,*

but have everlasting life."

So we will not "spend" Christmas…

nor observe Christmas.

We will "keep" Christmas—keep it as it is…

in all the loveliness of its ancient traditions.

May we keep it in our hearts,

that we may be kept in its hope.

—Peter Marshall—

FEZZIWEG'S BALL

Old Fezziweg laid down his pen, and looked up at the clock, which pointed to the hour of seven. He rubbed his hands; adjusted his capacious waistcoat; laughed all over himself, from his shoes to his organ of benevolence; and called out in a comfortable, oily, rich, fat, jovial voice:

"Yo, ho, there! Ebenezer! Dick! Yo, ho, my boys!" said Fezziweg, "no more work tonight. Christmas Eve, Dick! Christmas Ebenezer! Let's have the shutters up," cried old Fezziweg, with a sharp clap of his hands, "before a man can say Jack Robinson!"

You wouldn't believe how those two fellows went at it! They charged into the street with the shutters—one, two, three—had 'em up in their places—four, five, six— barred 'em and pinned 'em— seven, eight, nine—and came back before you could have got to twelve, panting like race-horses.

"Hilli-ho!" cried old Fezziweg, skipping down from the high desk with wonderful agility. "Clear away, my lads, and let's have lots of room here! Hilli-ho Dick! Chirrup, Ebenezer!"

Clear away! There was nothing they wouldn't have cleared away, or couldn't have cleared away, with old Fezziweg looking on. It was done in a minute.

Every movable was packed off, as if it were dismissed from public life forever-more; the floor was swept and watered, the lamps were trimmed, fuel was heaped upon the fire; and the warehouse was as snug, and as warm, and dry, and bright a ball-room, as you would desire to see upon a winter's night.

In came a fiddler with a music-book, and went up to the lofty desk, and made an orchestra of it, and turned like fifty stomach-aches. In came Mrs. Fezziweg, one vast substantial smile. In came the three Miss Fezziwegs, beaming and lovable. In came the six young followers whose hearts they broke. In came all the young men and women employed in the business. In came the housemaid, with her cousin, the baker.

In came the cook, with her brother's particular friend, the milkman. In came the boy from over the way, who was suspected of not having board enough from his master; trying to hide himself behind the girl from next door but one, who was proved to have had her ears pulled by her mistress. In they all came, one after another; some shyly, some boldly, some gracefully, some awkwardly, some pushing, some pulling; in they all came, anyhow and everyhow. Away they all went, twenty couples at once; hands half round and back again the other way; down the middle and up again; round and round in various stages of affectionate grouping; old top couple always turning up in the wrong place; new top couple starting off again, as soon as they got there; all top couples at last, and not a bottom one to help them.

When this result was brought about, old Fezziweg, clapping his hands to stop the dance, cried out, "Well done!" and the fiddler plunged his hot face into a pot of porter, especially provided for that purpose. But scoring rest upon his reappearance, he instantly began again, though there were no dancers yet, as if the other fiddler had been carried home, exhausted, on a shutter, and he were a brand-new man determined to beat him out of sight, or perish.

There were more dances, and there were more forfeits, and more dances, and there was a cake, and there was a great piece of Cold Roast, and there was a great piece of Cold Boiled, and there were mincepies, and plenty of beer. But the great effect of the evening came after the Roast and Boiled when the fiddler struck up *"Sir Roger de Coverley."* Then old Fezziweg stood out to dance with Mrs. Fezziweg. Top couple, too who were not to be trifled with; people who would dance, and had no notion of walking.

But if there had been twice as many partners old Fezziweg would have been a match for them, and so would Mrs. Fezziweg. She was worthy to be his partner in every sense of the term.

A positive light appeared to issue from Fezziweg's calves. They shone in every part of the dance like moons. You couldn't have predicted, at any given time, what would become of them next. And when old Fezziweg and Mrs. Fezziweg had gone all through the dance; advance and retire, both hands to your partner, bow and curtsy,

corkscrew, thread the needle, and back again to your place, Fezziweg "cut" so deftly that he appeared to wink with his legs, and came upon his feet again without a stagger.

When the clock struck eleven, this domestic ball broke up. Mr. and Mrs. Fezziweg took their stations, one on either side the door, and shaking hands with every person individually as he or she went out, wished him or her a Merry Christmas.

—*Charles Dickens*

THE MAN WHO MISSED CHRISTMAS

It was Christmas Eve, and as usual, George Mason was the last to leave the office. He walked over to a massive safe, spun the dials, swung the heavy door open. Making sure the door would not close behind him, he stepped inside.

A square of white cardboard was taped just above the topmost row of strongboxes. On the card a few words were written. George Mason stared at those words, remembering…

*   *   *   *   *   *   *   *   *   *

Exactly one year ago he had entered this selfsame vault. And then, behind his back, slowly, noiselessly, the ponderous door swung shut. He was trapped—entombed in the sudden and terrifying dark. He hurled himself at the unyielding door, his hoarse cry sounding like an explosion. Through his mind flashed all the stories he had heard of men found suffocated in time vaults. No time clock controlled his mechanism; the safe would remain locked until it was opened from the outside. Tomorrow morning. Then the realization hit him. No one would come tomorrow—tomorrow was Christmas.

Once more he flung himself at the door, shouting wildly, until he sank on his knees, exhausted. Silence came, high-pitched, singing silence that seemed deafening. More than thirty-six hours would pass before anyone came—thirty-six hours in a steel box three feet wide, eight feet long, seven feet high. Would the oxygen last?

Perspiring and breathing heavily, he felt his way around the floor. Then, in the far right-hand corner, just above the floor, he found a small, circular opening. Quickly he thrust his finger into it and felt, faint but unmistakable, a cool current of air. The tension release was so sudden that he burst into tears.

But at last he sat up. Surely he would not have to stay trapped for the full thirty-six hours. Somebody would miss him. But who? He was unmarried and lived alone. The maid who cleaned his apartment was just a servant; he had always treated her as such. He had been invited to spend Christmas Eve with his brother's family, but children got on his nerves, and expected presents. A friend had asked him to go to a home for elderly people on Christmas Day, and play the piano—George Mason was a good musician. But he had made some excuse or other; he had intended to sit at home with a good

cigar, listening to some new recordings he was giving himself. George Mason dug his nails into the palms of his hands until the pain balanced the misery in his mind. Nobody would come and let him out. Nobody, nobody… Miserably the whole of Christmas Day went by, and the succeeding night.

On the morning after Christmas the head clerk came into the office at the usual time, opened the safe, and then went on into his private office. No one saw George Mason stagger out into the corridor, run to the water cooler, and drink great gulps of water. No one paid any attention to him as he left and took a taxi home. There he shaved, changed his wrinkled clothes, ate breakfast and returned to his office, where his employees greeted him casually. That day he met several acquaintances and talked to his own brother. Grimly, inexorably, the truth closed in on George Mason. He had vanished from human society during the great festival of brotherhood; no one had missed him at all.

Reluctantly, George Mason began to think about the true meaning of Christmas. Was it possible that he had been blind all these years with selfishness, indifference, pride? Wasn't giving, after all the essence of Christmas because it marked the time God gave His own Son to the world? All through the year that followed, with little hesitant deeds of kindness, with small, unnoticed acts of unselfishness, George Mason tried to prepare himself…

*   *   *   *   *   *   *   *   *   *

Now, once more, it is Christmas Eve. Slowly he backs out of the safe, closes it. He touches its grim steel face lightly, almost affectionately, and leaves the office. There he goes now in his black overcoat and hat, the same George Mason as a year ago. Or is it? He walks a few blocks, then flags a taxi, anxious not to be late. His nephews are expecting him to help them trim the tree. Afterwards, he is taking his brother and his sister-in-law to a Christmas play. Why is he so happy? Why does this jostling against others, laden as he is with bundles, exhilarate, and delight him? Perhaps the card has something to do with it, the card he taped inside his office safe last New Year's Day. On the card is written in George Mason's own hand:

To love people, to be indispensable somewhere, that is the purpose of life. That is the secret of happiness.

—J.Edgar Park

THE CHRISTMAS PAGEANT

Our church had not had a full-blown Christmas pageant in years. For one thing, we had become fairly rational and efficient about the season, content to let the Sunday School observe the event on their own turf in a low-key way. Then, too, there was the last time we had gone all out. That week of the Christmas pageant coincided with an outbreak of German measles, chicken pox, and the Hong Kong flu. The night of the pageant there was a sleet storm, a partial power failure that threw some people's clocks off, and one of the sheep hired for the occasion made a mess. That was about par for the course, since Joseph and two Wise Men upchucked during the performance and some little angels managed to both cry and wet their pants. To top it off, the choir of teenagers walking about in an irresponsible manner with lighted candles created more a feeling of the fear of fire and the wrath of God than a feeling of peace on earth. I don't think it was really all that bad, and maybe all those things didn't happen the same year, but a sufficient number of senior ladies in the church had had it up to here with the whole hoo-ha and tended to squelch any suggestion of another pageant. It was as if cholera had once again been amongst us and nobody wanted to go through that again.

But nostalgia is strong, and it addled the brains of those same senior ladies as they considered the pleas of the younger mothers who had not been through this ritual ordeal and would not be dissuaded. It was time their children had their chance.

And in short order, people who kept saying "I ought to know better" were right in there making angel costumes out of old bedsheets, cardboard, and chicken feathers. Just the right kind of bathrobes could not be found for the Wise Men, so some of the daddies went out and bought new ones and backed a pickup truck over them to age them a bit. One of the young mothers was pregnant, and it was made clear to her in loving terms that she was expected to come up with a real newborn child by early December. She vowed to try.

An angel choir was lashed into singing shape. A real manger with real straw was obtained. And while there was a consensus on leaving out live sheep this time, some enterprising soul managed to borrow two small goats for the evening. The real coup was renting a live donkey for the Mother Mary to ride in on. None of us had ever seen a live

donkey ridden through a church chancel, and it seemed like such a fine thing to do at the time.

We made one concession to sanity, deciding to have the thing on a Sunday morning in the full light of day, so we could see what we were doing and nobody in the angel choir would get scared of the dark and cry or wet their pants. No candles, either. And no full rehearsal. These things are supposed to be a little hokey, anyhow, and nobody was about to go through the whole thing twice.

The great day came and everybody arrived at church. Husbands who were not known for regular attendance came—probably for the same reason they would be attracted to a nearby bus wreck.

It wasn't all that bad, really. At least, not early on. The goats did get loose in the parking lot and put on quite a rodeo with the shepherds. But we hooted out the carols with full voice, and the angel choir got through its first big number almost on key and in unison. The Star of Bethlehem was lit over the manger, and it came time for the entrance of Joseph and Mary, with Mary riding on the U-Haul donkey, carrying what later proved to be a rag doll (since the pregnant lady was overdue). It was the donkey that proved our undoing.

The donkey made two hesitant steps through the door of the chancel, took a look at the whole scene, and seized up. Locked his legs, put his whole body in a cement condition well beyond rigor mortis, and the procession ground to a halt. Now there are things you might consider doing in private to get it to move, but there is a limit to what you can do to a donkey in church on a Sunday morning in front of women and children. Jerking on his halter and some wicked kicking on the part of the Virgin Mary had no effect.

The president of the board of trustees, seated in the front row and dressed in his Sunday best, rose to the rescue. The floor of the chancel was polished cement. And so, with another man pulling at the halter, the president of the board crouched at the stern end of the donkey and pushed—slowing sliding the rigid beast across the floor, inch by stately inch. With progress being made, the choir director turned on the tape recorder, which blared forth a mighty chorus from the Mormon Tabernacle Choir accompanied by the Philadelphia Orchestra.

Just as the donkey and his mobilizers reached mid-church, the tape recorder blew a

fuse and there was a sudden silence. And in that silence an exasperated voice came from the backside of the donkey. "Just move it!" Followed immediately by a voice from the rear of the church—the donkey pusher's wife—"Leon, shut your mouth!" And that's when the donkey brayed. We are such fun to watch when we do what we do.

It has been several years since the church has held another Christmas pageant, but we have not seen the last one. The memory of the laughter outlives the memory of the hassle. And hope—hope always makes us believe that this time, this year, we will get it right. That's the whole deal with Christmas, I guess. It's just real life—only a lot more of it all at once than usual.

And I suppose we will continue doing it all. Get frenzied and confused and frustrated and even mad. And also get excited and hopeful and quietly pleased. We will laugh and cry and pout and ponder. Get a little foolish and excessive. Hug and kiss and make a great mess. Spend too much. And somebody will always be there to upchuck or wet their pants. As always, we will sing only some of the verses and most of those off-key. We will do it again and again and again. We are the Christmas pageant—the whole darn thing. And I think it's best to just let it happen. As at least one person I know can attest, getting pushy about it is trouble.

—*Robert Fulghum*

Ring Out the Old

Ring out the old, ring in the new;
Ring, happy bells, across the snow;
The year is going, let him go;
Ring out the false, ring in the true.

Ring out the grief that saps the mind,
For those that here we see no more;
Ring out the feud of rich and poor,
Ring in redress to all mankind.

Ring out false pride in place and blood,
The civic slander and the spite;
Ring in the love of truth and right,
Ring in the common love of good.

Ring in the valiant man and free,
The larger heart, the kindlier hand;
Ring out darkness of the land,
Ring in the Christ that is to be.

—Alfred, Lord Tennyson—